Dedicated to
Janice & Jordan
For their support and smiles

Colorado

FINE ART LANDSCAPE & NATURE PHOTOGRAPHY

Photography and Text

By

David L. Clack

Published by Colorado Photographics, Inc.
Fort Collins, Colorado

ISBN 0-9666786-0-5

Library of Congress Catalog Number: 94-73495

FIRST EDITION

FOURTH PRINTING

Published by Colorado Photographics, Inc.

P.O. Box 270874 Fort Collins, Colorado 80527

www.coloradophotographics.com

Printed in Hong Kong by C&C Offset Printing Co., Ltd.

First Photo: Fall Splendor, Along Maroon Creek Road

Opposite Page: Moss & Rock, Maroon Creek

Introduction

As a young boy I would hike and camp throughout the Colorado wilderness. I marvelled at the beauty and purity of it all: the crisp clean air and the sound of wind rustling through the tops of Ponderosa pine. Growing older I wondered: "Where did all this come from, how could something so beautiful exist?" In the back of my mind I knew it was God's creation, yet I suppressed those thoughts, not wanting to deal with the confrontation of God's existence and mine.

Now as an adult, I have reconciled my separation from God through Jesus Christ, my Lord and Savior, through whom all things are possible. So, it is my joy and honor to thank Him who has made the culmination of these images possible for you to enjoy.

–David L. Clack

"You are worthy, our Lord and God, to receive glory and honor and power, for You created all things. . ."

Rev. 4:11

Opposite Page: Yankee Boy Basin

Preface

As the golden rays of sunlight begin to light up the clouds above, and then the jagged mountain tops, I wait anxiously for just the right moment. If I wait too long, the contrast between mountains and foreground will be greater than the film is capable of handling.

Click, I gently squeeze my cable release. Exposures can be several seconds long, so I am careful not to jiggle the camera. Quickly, I turn the film holder around and shoot another and then another or as many shots as I can fire off. Sometimes my window of opportunity is just for a few minutes. If I had not scouted out the right location the night before, I might have spent too much time composing the image and miss the shot altogether. After all, I am looking at an image that is projected onto ground glass, upside down, backwards and barely visible under my focusing cloth.

Light is everything. It is the key to any landscape photograph. How it plays upon the landscape can make the difference between success or failure. So many times I have awakened at four or five o'clock in the morning, hiked up to a spot with 50 pounds of camera gear on my back, realizing as dawn

Opposite Page: Aspen Grove, Crystal Colorado

approaches, that the sky is completely clouded over. With no chance of getting that spectacular sunrise I had anticipated, I have to regroup and look elsewhere for a potential photograph. A close-up of Columbine protruding out of lichen covered rocks would make an ideal shot with softer light.

Although sunrise and sunset are generally considered the best times of the day to shoot, some of my better work has been during midday. A lot depends on the light: is it cloudy or sunny, stormy or calm? I never know from one minute to the next what Colorado weather will bring, especially in the mountains. It can change in an instant. What may seem a hopeless situation one minute, can turn into a perfect opportunity the next.

Whether hiking up a long and arduous trail or driving along one of the many scenic by-ways, I always delight in discovering new vistas I had not seen before. It is a joy and a privilege to be able to photograph the many facets of Colorado. My goal as a nature photographer is to capture on film an image that is aesthetically pleasing to the eye, and also captures the mood and emotion experienced while I was there. It is my hope that you will also experience that same joy.

–D.C.

Opposite Page: Fall Colors, Weston Pass

The San Juan Mountains

Summertime: the San Juan Mountains of Uncompahgre National Forest provide a beautiful array of lush wildflowers blanketing the meadows and basins. Majestic snowcapped peaks tower above the valleys below, creating stunning vistas. During the Fall, golden Aspen light up the hillsides with an incredible display of late September color. Located in the southwest region of Colorado, the San Juan Mountains are without question one of the more scenic areas in the state.

Flowers & Mountains, Mount Sneffels Range

Old Fence, Dallas Divide Road, San Juan Mountains

Yankee Boy Basin

Columbine, American Basin

Opposite Page: Fireweed, Yankee Boy Basin

Wolcott Mountain, Mount Sneffels Wilderness

Columbine & Lichen, American Basin

Early Morning, Mt. Sneffels Wilderness

Sunrise, Indian Paintbrush, American Basin

Rocky Mountain National Park

In 1915, with the help of Enos Mills, a naturalist and conservationist, Rocky Mountain National Park was founded. From the fragile alpine tundra of Trail Ridge Road to the many meadows, lakes and meandering streams, such as Moraine Park, Bear Lake and Tyndall Creek, the park is an ideal setting for nature photography.

Above Dream Lake, Tyndall Creek

Morning Light, Moraine Park

Sunrise, Halett Peak, Bear Lake

Wild Flowers, Trail Ridge Road

Sunrise, Sprague Lake, Hallett Peak

Winter Snow, Fall River Road

Impending Storm, Trail Ridge Road

Garden
of the Gods

Brilliantly colored sandstone monoliths towering above ancient Juniper trees, contrasted against deep azure blue skies, the Garden of the Gods is unique unto itself. With such intriguing rock formations, one does not have to look far to visualize dramatic compositions. Located outside Colorado Springs, it is easily accessible by foot or car.

Opposite Page: Sunrise, Siamese Twins

Sunset Silhouette

Siamese Twins & Pike's Peak

Kissing Camels & Juniper, Garden of the Gods

Sunrise, South Gateway Rock

Roosevelt National Forest

Immense granite mountains rise gracefully above glaciated valleys and dense forests of Douglas fir, Ponderosa and Lodgepole pine. Creeks and trails meander back and forth through the backcountry. Roosevelt National Forest, with its diverse landscape, offers an abundance of photographic opportunities. Originally named Colorado National Forest in 1910, it was renamed after President Theodore Roosevelt in 1932.

Cameron Pass, Near Lake Agnes

Winter Sunset, Rawah Wilderness

Twin Sisters Mountain, Estes Park

Gunnison National Forest

There are several locations throughout Colorado that offer prolific wildflowers. The area around Crested Butte of Gunnison National Forest is one of those places. The delicate beauty of Wild Asters and Lupine, along with Fireweed, Columbine and other wildflowers frolicking in the wind, articulates in images the purity of nature.

Wild Asters Along The Gunnison River

Lupine, Cottonwood Pass

Old Miner's Cabin, Crystal

Mount Owen, Ruby Range

Dead Horse Mill, Crystal

Morning Reflection, Ruby Range

Sunrise, Whetstone Mountain, Crested Butte

The Front Range
& Eastern Plains

Mountains and plains meet, and streams turn into rivers, etching out the last bit of land, creating deep gorges and canyons. A lone tree stands out in the middle of a vast prairie, enduring the frigid cold of winter. The front range and eastern plains are often some of the most overlooked places to photograph. Their surprising beauty is unsurpassed anywhere.

Frosted Cottonwood

Poudre River, Fort Collins

Big Thompson Canyon

Pike
National Forest

Teeming with brilliant color, some of the most prolific groves of Aspen can be found near South Park in Pike National Forest. The vibrancy of the Aspen tree adds a sophisticated elegance to the landscape. A prime example is along the Colorado Trail at Kenosha Pass. Such timeless visions express the aesthetic beauty of the Colorado landscape.

Aspen, Kenosha Pass, Colorado Trail

White River National Forest

On the fringe of the Maroon Bells-Snowmass Wilderness in White River National Forest, lie the Maroon Bells. Whether it be the soft pastels of a predawn reflection or the vivid, crisp colors from the mid-morning sun, it is easy to understand why this is one of the most photographed places in all of Colorado. Located just outside Aspen, first impressions of this area are absolutely breathtaking.

Previous Overleaf: Aspen Grove, Conifer

Reflection, Maroon Bells   57

Moss Covered Rock- Maroon Creek, Aspen Colorado

Aspen & Sky, Along Maroon Creek Road

Beaver Dams, Maroon Bells

Fall Foliage, Near Maroon Bells

Eagles Nest Wilderness

In the midst of White River and Arapahoe National Forest lies Eagles Nest Wilderness. Here the Gore Range eloquently stands high above cascading waterfalls and subalpine lakes as they glisten with the freshly melted snow of the past winter. Eagles Nest Wilderness can be accessed from either side of the Gore Range. Which ever way you choose, this is definitely a trek worth the effort.

Sunrise, Eagles Nest Peak

Indian Paintbrush & Blue Spruce

Cascading Stream, Eagles Nest Wilderness

Acknowledgements

I would like to express my appreciation to my parents, Frank and Edith, over the years their love and encouragement have been instrumental in the success of my career, to Ed Donner, Bill Eck, Dale Hetherington and especially my dad who have given me insight and companionship as they accompanied me on various photo excursions, to John Dubler, Janice Clack and Lois Hopple for their help with editing and to my family and friends whose uplifting words have contributed towards the making of this book.

Stones & Reflection, Poudre River

Technical Info

All photographs, with the exception of one image, were taken with a Toyo 45A II 4x5 field camera. For *Columbine, American Basin* I used a 6x6 Hasselblad.

My film of choice is Fuji Provia, ASA 100. With a few images I used Ektachrome ASA 100. *Fall Colors, Weston Pass* and *Aspen, Kenosha Pass* were taken with Pro 100 negative film. I almost always shoot negative and transparency films of each image with the exception of my early work where I only shot negatives. Transparencies usually work best for offset printing and negatives for original C prints.

Exposures ranged from 1/125 of a second to 12 seconds. I tried to shoot around F22, (the mid-aperture range in large format), to minimize inherent lens aberrations. However, with many of my images, I was down to an F45 or F64 aperture to maximize depth of field.

The photographs in this book are available as original fine art prints.
Contact Colorado Photographics for details.

P.O. Box 270874 Fort Collins, Colorado 80527
www.coloradophotographics.com